GW00703189

The Sermon on the Mount

Living the Jesus Way

Paul Smith

A m∈t Publication

Published for m∈t by

MOORLEY'S Print & Publishing

ISBN 978-086071-612-0

British Library Cataloguing in Publication Data.
A catalogue record for this book is available
from the British Library.

MET PUBLICATIONS

are published for MET by

MOORLEY'S Print & Publishing
23 Park Rd., Ilkeston, Derbys DE7 5DA
⊃◯ Tel/Fax: (0115) 932 0643 ◯⊂

Contents

The Sermon on the Mount

Introduction
Matthew 5: 1-2

The Sermon on the Mount is undoubtedly one of the most influential passages of Scripture. Even by unbelievers, the value of its teaching is widely acclaimed. Like children peering through a letter box, we catch a glimpse of the lifestyle and ethical principles which, Jesus says, apply amongst His followers in His kingdom.

Yet no one can read the Sermon on the Mount without feeling the challenge of its teaching. Whilst some passages speak a word of comfort to a troubled soul, others are profoundly disturbing. At times Jesus seems to take principles, which are already difficult to keep, and make them even harder. Yet, deep within we all recognise that the world would be a different, and much better place, if everyone lived according to this teaching.

Before we embark upon a detailed study, it is important to recognise the context in which Matthew places the teaching in the ministry of Jesus. As chapter 5 opens, we are reminded, contrary to the view often held, that the teaching is for the disciples alone. Indeed it was when Jesus saw the crowds that the disciples came to Him from the crowd to receive this teaching. It is as though Jesus is saying, 'Here is a picture of how you are to live. This is not how the world lives'.

Nor must we forget the significance of mountains in Scripture. So often in the religious history of these Jewish people, God had been encountered on the mountain. One immediately thinks of Elijah on Mount Carmel and, more significantly for us, Moses on Mount Sinai. These first followers of Jesus, Jews to a man, could not have failed to notice the significance of this, nor could Matthew as he compiled his Gospel. It seems as though the Sermon on the Mount is the New Testament parallel to the giving of the Law on Mount Sinai. One might fairly assume that here we are dealing with the New Covenant equivalent of the Law under the Old Covenant.

So, we begin to reflect upon the ethical teaching of Jesus, given specifically to those who have responded to the call of discipleship.

The Disciples' Character

The Beatitudes
Matthew 5: 3-12

It is maybe helpful, initially, to recognise that these great verses concern Christian character. They are about our attitudes. They are the 'be–attitudes'. In many, both traditional and modern translations, they each begin with the word 'blessed'; not the most familiar word in the 21st century. Recognizing this difficulty, some translations use the word 'happy', which is fine as long as we recognise that Jesus is using the word in a very distinctive way. It would be entirely wrong for us to believe that Jesus was talking about happiness in the way the world understands it. Here there is nothing superficial. The happiness, which Jesus, describes is not dependent upon circumstances. Rather, it is a deep sense of well-being and contentment, which finds its spring in the soul, and is able to keep us whatever we have to face.

Happiness of this kind is exactly what the world is looking for. Any reflection on the profusion of spiritualities to be found in modern society, and the extraordinary lengths to which people go in pursuing them, leave us in no doubt that people are looking for this deep sense of inner contentment. But here's the surprise: the source of happiness, according to Jesus, are the very things that people are running away from. Poverty of spirit, mourning, meekness, etc. are the very things that people try to avoid. Indeed the popular notion is that happiness is not to be found in these kinds of attitudes at all, but rather in making your mark, being assertive, and letting other people know that you are around. These are the things that modern society tells us lead to success and happiness. Nothing could be further from the truth, as Jesus tells it.

Then where is this happiness to be found? Jesus' answer is that it concerns the life of the spirit. These things are essentially spiritual qualities. Before thinking about each one individually, we need to make two observations. Firstly, it is wrong to imagine that Jesus speaks of eight different groups of people, each one exhibiting one of these qualities. On the contrary, these qualities, Jesus expects, are to be found in every disciple. Even a cursory examination of them convinces us of this truth. We are all expected to be people who hunger and thirst for righteousness, are merciful, have purity of heart, and so on.

Secondly, it is quite wrong to imagine that Jesus gives us a list arranged in a haphazard manner, just a miscellaneous collection of the kind of qualities He expects to see in His followers. As we shall see, they are arranged in a progressive order, beginning with poverty of spirit, and ascending step by step to the kind of faith which faces persecution for righteousness' sake. They are an ascending staircase, a kind of route-map for those who would travel the road of discipleship.

Our journey begins with spiritual poverty. That is where every true disciple must begin. It is the only embarkation point for this journey. We cannot make this journey if we think we know how to do it. We can only begin with the spiritual poverty which acknowledges that we do not have what it takes to be the people God intends us to be. Search for happiness as I may, my quest will be unfulfilled if I think that by my effort I can attain it. Yet the miracle is that it can begin to be mine as soon as I admit that I can't do it. That is the spiritual poverty of which Jesus is here speaking. And mark the promise. Once I admit how spiritually poor I am, indeed spiritually bankrupt without Christ, then the promise is that the kingdom of heaven can be mine.

That kind of self-realization, especially amongst those who have tried to find happiness for many years, is a very painful thing. Mourning is about a sense of emptiness and loss. When we realise our own emptiness without Christ, mourning is an obvious reaction. We are deeply saddened by our own condition. Yet the Saviour will not leave us in that condition, for the promise is that we shall be comforted.

Meekness must not be confused with weakness. Meekness is about humble submission to a higher authority, and it marks the next step on this ascending journey. Once we realise our spiritual bankruptcy, and mourn our condition, we need to recognise, not only that that is the state we are in, but also that we can't get ourselves out of it. We long for happiness and contentment. We recognise how bankrupt we are. We mourn our condition, and then we need, with a meek heart, to recognise that if ever things are going to be different, it will not be because of what we do, but because of what is done for us. Once we recognise that, the promise of Jesus is that we will inherit the earth. As Charles Wesley taught us to sing: 'Jesus and all in Him is mine'.

Yet this meek acknowledgment that we do not have what it takes does not diminish our desire. On the contrary, it increases it. We catch a vision of a new kind of life. We long for the life of holiness. We hunger and thirst for righteousness. Far from depressing us, this increased hunger is a sign of spiritual health. A good appetite is a clear indicator of health. This is spiritually true as well. In a prosperous western society like ours, words like hunger and thirst have often lost their cutting edge; not so for the first followers of Jesus. They knew what it was to both hunger and thirst. Now, when there is that same kind of intense desire for righteousness, Jesus promises that the thirst will be quenched, the hunger satisfied, and we shall be filled.

At this point on the journey, realizing our own bankruptcy and helplessness, glimpsing the life of righteousness, and realizing how far short we have fallen, it is natural to recognise that we all stand in need of the mercy of God. How can it be ours? How can we be shown mercy? Such is reserved, Jesus says, for those who themselves have such a humble attitude that they are merciful to others. Just as we will never know the kingdom, nor will we inherit the earth whilst we think we can do it, we shall never receive the mercy of God when we cherish in our own hearts a self-assertive attitude, or even worse, one that exacts revenge on those who have wronged us. As Jesus pointed out in other places, a merciful attitude is the key to knowing the mercy of God.

Purity of heart marks the next step. For something to be pure it needs to be unadulterated and unalloyed. The heart is, in Scripture, descriptive of the seat of one's emotions and character. Consequently, purity of heart is about single-mindedness or 'single-heartedness'. This makes us ask all sorts of questions about our focus on the life of discipleship. So often we want this, but we want the rest as well. Yet the promise of Jesus is that with heart entirely focused on this one thing, we shall see God. We might just observe that this is not just a promise for the future. It is the normal experience of the sanctified soul. Think of some of the great saints who have gone before us. They saw God everywhere and in everything.

When, with a single eye, we desire this one thing, and when we begin to see God at work, it is not surprising that we begin to share in His work of reconciliation. So much conflict is caused by intrigue and deceit. It is completely understandable, therefore, that those with a pure heart should be peacemakers. As we are adopted into His family, becoming His sons, we share in His work of reconciliation.

It would be folly to believe that the world would hail and welcome such people with open arms. Not so. They belong to another kingdom with another set of values, which are opposed to the values of the world. And it is not surprising, therefore, that they will be persecuted. The cause of their persecution will be their righteousness. They will stand out in contrast to the world around them, and the world will hate them. But they will be happy and content, resting in the divine will, and there will be deep in their hearts something that the world cannot take away, and cannot touch. It is the Kingdom of Heaven.

One can imagine the shock of the disciples at this point in Jesus' sermon. Up until this time the disciples could be excused for thinking that Jesus was talking about others. But now He makes clear what lies ahead for everyone who is counted as His disciple. There will be insult, persecution, malice, and all kinds of evil. But how are they to react? They are to rejoice and be glad. They have found something that the world has missed, despite all its searching. No one can take that away from them. They stand in a great line of those who have gone before, and who have similarly been persecuted. And they know that one day heaven will be theirs.

The disciple of Jesus belongs to another kingdom. The world may prize power, wealth, prestige, and popularity, but the Christian disciple lets it all wash over him. He takes the standards of another kingdom. He will not let the world push him into its mould. As Dietrich Bonhoeffer (who died for his faith under Nazi tyranny) wrote: "With every Beatitude the gulf is widened between the disciple and the people, and their call to come forth from the people becomes increasingly manifest".

The disciple belongs to another world, where the last is first, where the people at the bottom finish up at the top, and where those who know they have nothing finish up gaining the whole world. That's the kingdom that I want to belong to. How about you?

The Disciples' Influence

Salt and Light
Matthew 5: 13-16

Jesus' focus in the Beatitudes on Christian character must not lead us to believe that discipleship is an entirely private matter between the individual and his Lord. On the contrary, it is the intention of Jesus that the lives of disciples should have an effect on the lives of those who are not yet disciples. The focus on Christian character, therefore, leads naturally to Christian influence.

If we were to read the Beatitudes without a commitment to Christian discipleship we may find ourselves admiring the character described, but we would find it difficult to believe that such characters could have any influence at all. Indeed, the world's view is that those who influence the lives of others most are those whose character is quite opposite to the one described in the Beatitudes. Here we have just another example of the way in which the life of discipleship is radically different from the life of the world.

This distinction is one which needs to be maintained. In both these metaphors Jesus emphasizes the distinction. Further, any influence which the disciple is to have will depend upon the distinction being maintained. We cease to influence the world if we are assimilated into it. Jesus' picture of the life of a disciple is one in which the disciple is quite different from those who are not disciples, living under a different value system. Yet the clear implication of Jesus' teaching is that the earth needs the salt, and the world is a dark place in which the disciple is intended to shine.

If we are to get to the heart of this teaching we need to be asking ourselves what salt and light do, for that is what our Christian influence ought to be. But even that question is not enough for we remember that the society in which Jesus lived is very different from ours, so we need to be asking what salt and light meant there. This is where we will get a clearer picture of Jesus' intention for us.

Today, salt is used most commonly for flavouring. It is sprinkled, not too much, to bring out the flavour of the dish. Whilst there may be some truth in this, we will only get to the heart of the teaching by recognizing that salt fulfilled very different functions in the society in which Jesus lived. There, unlike us today, they had no refrigerators. Being a hot climate the question of how food was to be preserved was a very real one. Their answer was that it would be preserved by being salted. The salt stopped the meat going off. It prevented decomposition setting in.

Salt had another very important use in Jesus' society. Without the benefit of a drainage system or flush toilets, salt was used as a disinfectant. Its antiseptic qualities were prized. How easy it would have been for infection to spread in unsanitary conditions. Salt was the answer. Somehow it killed harmful bacteria and stopped infection spreading.

What a powerful picture this is of the Christian's life. As Christians are sprinkled through society it is the intention of Jesus that they will stop society degenerating, going off, and they will also have a kind of disinfectant quality. As they are scattered throughout the earth their moral purity will kill the potential for moral infection setting in.

The idea of salt losing its saltiness is a puzzle to many. In fact, if we think of the salt we have in our kitchens we could reasonably say that it is impossible for it to lose its saltiness. So what did Jesus mean? This is where it is helpful to remember how Jesus' contemporaries got their salt. It would not be mined or refined like the salt we get today, but often it would be gathered from the shoreline of the Dead Sea. It is easy to understand how, when it was collected, dirt and sand were collected with it. Altogether they would be shovelled up and taken away to be used, for example, in disinfecting the toilets. Now let us imagine that outside the toilet block there was a pile of salt, and a small shovel with which it would be scattered when the toilet had been used. And let's imagine that it rained heavily. What would happen? The salt itself would dissolve and wash away. All that would remain in the pile would be the debris that had been collected with it. That is of no use for disinfecting. It's only use is to be thrown on the road to fill a pot hole or provide a footpath.

What a powerful picture this is. If Christians lose that which makes them distinctively different, if they become assimilated in the society they are meant to influence, if their value systems are not distinctively different, and their faith is not real any potential for influence is lost. They can no longer fill the Master's intention. One of the great tragedies of the Church in every generation is that those who were meant to be society's saviours become society's footpath.

If Jesus' society had neither refrigerators nor flushed toilets, it is also helpful to remember that they did not have street lights either. There was no electricity in the home, and once night fell everything depended upon the light from an oil lamp. How difficult it is for us living in a bright world like ours to imagine what life in Jesus' society must have been like. There the light which a lamp gave was of crucial importance. It enabled life to go on in dark places. If one had to travel at night one depended upon the light from the lamp which was carried. If people did not immediately go to bed when dusk fell, everything in the home depended upon the lamp light.

Jesus, who later in St. John's Gospel would describe himself as 'The Light of the World', here speaks of His disciples being just that. The world is a dark place where people can easily stumble and fall, where injuries can easily happen, and where people find themselves groping in the darkness, unclear of the way ahead. Yet into this dark place Christians are sent to be light.

What a crazy thing it is to light a lamp and put it under a bowl! What a crazy thing it is to be a disciple of Jesus, and to be shut away from the world that He intends us to influence.

Those who would be, like their Master, the light of the world, are meant to be placed strategically where the light they bring will have the maximum effect. Furthermore, in just the same way that the lights of a city have an unmistakable identity and brilliance on a dark night, so when Christians gather together there should be something which emanates from their gathering and influences others for good, stops them falling, helps them not to get lost, and guides them safely home.

What is it which should emanate from this gathered source of light? The answer is goodness or, as Jesus put it, good deeds. So the powerful image which Jesus is giving us is that as disciples whose character is shaped by the Beatitudes live out the goodness of God, they will be like lamps burning brightly in a dark place. Yet they will covet no praise for themselves, but rather rejoice when their Father in heaven is praised for the good deeds which they do.

Disciples must not fail the world they are called to serve. We are to be what God is making us. We must not lose our saltiness, or hide our light, but rather like salt which is scattered we can purify and disinfect society, and like light which is burning brightly, and sometimes gathered with other lights, we can guide and enable those around us to find the right path. Yet we need to remember that both salt and light fulfil their purpose by giving themselves. Salt is ineffective unless it is given to that which it should influence. The lamp only burns brightly as the oil is consumed. We ought not to be surprised that if God so loved the world that He gave, and if Jesus so loved that He gave, we also ought to expect to give ourselves in love to others and for others. This is the way the world will be influenced, and this is the way God will be glorified.

The Disciples' Conduct
Matthew 5: 17-48

The Fulfilment of the Law
Matthew 5: 17-20

Having spoken about Christian character and Christian influence, Jesus is about to address the whole issue of Christian conduct. He will focus on a number of issues which were pertinent for those who first heard Him, and are just as important for us today.

Before dealing with specific situations, because the Law was so important for His first hearers, Jesus deals specifically with this. It was and is a real issue. We, like those first disciples, find ourselves in a dilemma. On the one hand we believe that God has made His will clear in the Law, and on the other hand we recognise that not one single person has ever kept the Law. Every page of the Old Testament speaks of failure. One can imagine how, with this background, and aware of the radical nature of Jesus' teaching, those first disciples hoped that He had come to abolish the Law completely; to set them free from having to keep its demands. Jesus clearly says that this is not the case. He has not come to abolish the Law, but to fulfil it. Indeed, in a way that is surprising to us and that must have shocked those first disciples, He seems to underline the importance of the Law. It is important, not just to keep the Law, but to encourage others to do so as well. Far from ruling out the Law, Jesus clearly rules it in.

There is a deeper question which demands our attention. If God knew that no one would ever keep the Law, why did He give it? It seems so unfair as though God, knowing human weakness and failure, was placing an impossible burden on people. Without doubt this is what the Law had become for Jesus' contemporaries, an impossible burden. From our perspective, the way the Law ordered every detail of human life seems like impossible legalism. We find it difficult to imagine how God could have required this.

We therefore need to be clear in our understanding. God gave the Law and yet, of course, He was aware that people would not be able to keep it. Then why did He give it? The answer is so that people would know that they needed a Saviour. To try and reach God's standards in our own strength is quite impossible, but we begin to be the people Christ intends us to be as we recognise our own failure. We simply cannot do it. We need someone to come and rescue and save us. In that sense the whole of the Old Testament was a preparation for the coming of Christ, the Saviour of the world.

Furthermore, we must recognise that in the paragraphs which follow Jesus uses a familiar formula. It is to be found in verses 21, 27, 31, 33, 38, and 43: "You have heard that it was said ... but I tell you". What is Jesus doing here? Firstly He is referring not so much to the written Law, as to the way that Law had been interpreted and applied. If He had been referring to the written Law the classic formula would have been, "It is written". But Jesus says, "You have heard that it was said". The Teachers of the Law had over the centuries taken the written Law, debated it at length, and worked out in the minutest detail how it should be applied in particular everyday situations. Because the Law was so difficult to keep the Scribes and Pharisees had sought to restrict the commands of the Law and extend the permissions which the Law gives in order to make it easier to keep. So the demands were less demanding and the permissions were more permissive after the Teachers of the Law had interpreted it. What Jesus deals with, therefore, is not so much the written Law as originally given, but the way it had been interpreted and applied by the religious leaders of the day. As we consider the following paragraphs we will see this very clearly. Of course, one of the motivating influences on the Scribes and the Pharisees was the desire to make the Law easier to keep for the religious elite, and more difficult for the rest. So, if you were prepared to subscribe to elaborate ritual you could find a way through, but if this was something you either did not or could not do, the Law was seen as condemning you.

What Jesus does here is to cut through the centuries of religious overlay, and get to the heart of the matter. He is not interested in making the Law less demanding, but in pointing out where the problem really lies. In each of the examples which follow, Jesus seeks to go behind the legalistic framework of the Law and address the cause. The problem in each case lies not in conduct but in motivation; not in what you do with your body but what inspires your heart.

Grasp these things, and we begin to understand what Jesus meant by not abolishing the Law and the Prophets, but fulfilling them. He is here enabling us to see that the end result of His ministry will be that ordinary people will be able to fulfil the Law because through the power of the Gospel they have been changed inside. Of course, this is in direct fulfilment of the Prophets. Jeremiah spoke of God putting the Law in people's minds and writing it on their hearts (Jeremiah 31:33). Ezekiel spoke of the Spirit of God at work in His people, moving them to follow God's decrees, and being careful to keep His laws (Ezekiel 36:27). For those who understand this background Jesus is clearly claiming to be the one who makes the fulfilment of the Law possible. He is holding out to people the possibility of living in a way that is pleasing and acceptable to God, not against one's will, but because our will is changed. The Law had become such a burden because people did not want to keep it. But the disciples of Jesus can know an inner transformation so that they live in harmony with God's will, not against their will, but because they want to do so. That is why their righteousness can surpass the righteousness of the Pharisees and the Teachers of the Law, and that is why, according to Jesus, they can enter the kingdom.

The Christian Faith, like the Jewish Law, can at its worst become a tremendous burden to carry. Instead of making us feel better, it can make us feel worse as though we are constant failures. Sometimes the disapproving attitude of someone in our churches compounds this situation. In our parents' generation people often put up with this. In our generation they will not. They will just walk away, and hundreds, maybe thousands, have. They have taken with them the impression that the Church is a collection of judgmental, disapproving hypocrites. They simply do not want to be part of something like that. The radical teaching of Jesus is, therefore, as pertinent for us today as it was for those who first heard it. Being a disciple is not about subscribing to a legalistic code, nor is it about saying that God's Law does not matter and I can do what I want. Jesus holds another possibility before us. It concerns setting His power free in the human heart where everything is first decided, being transformed there and, if that is renewed, there is a sense in which conduct looks after itself.

Living It Out
Matthew 5: 21-48

Jesus had not come to abolish the Law, so His followers have no right to say that there are no boundaries to Christian behaviour. Jesus had come to fulfil the Law, both in His teaching and supremely in a relationship with Him. His disciples can discover a way of living within the will of God. Indeed to live within the will of God will become the most important thing for them. As their relationship with Jesus grows their natural desire to live as they want will be replaced by a God given desire to live in harmony with their Master's will. The Law will be written on the heart. This is how we can fulfil it, not by getting away with as much as we can before the Law is actually broken, but by being transformed within so that God's will becomes ours.

In the following paragraphs Jesus applies this truth to different specific situations. They were pertinent in Jesus' society, and they are just as pertinent to us today.

Dealing with Anger
Matthew 5: 21-26

Whilst the direct command "Do not murder" is a quote from the written Law (Exodus 20: 13), the very fact that Jesus uses the phrase "You have heard that it was said" reminds us that we are dealing not just with the written Law, but the way in which it was interpreted. What the Scribes and Pharisees had done was to restrict the sin to the act of murder alone. This made the Law easier to obey. One only broke it when the life of another was actually taken.

On first reading Jesus seems to be making the Law even more difficult to keep. What He is actually doing is pointing out that the true application of this Law is not to restrict it to the act alone, but to recognise that it includes thoughts and words as well as deeds. Anger and insult are included as well as murder. One can understand why, because a murderous act begins with an angry thought, sometimes including insulting words. Jesus is going behind the letter of the Law to its spirit. It is not only the act of murder which is wrong, but angry thoughts and insulting words are also out of harmony with the will of God. The problem lies not in what is ultimately done, but in where that train of events began. The problem to be addressed is not simply in the actions committed, but in the desire within the heart.

In setting out a remedy Jesus uses two illustrations, one concerning worship in the Temple, and the other concerning litigation in the courts. In both, the emphasis lies in getting the relationship right. They are about reconciliation. Broken relationships need to be put right. In both these cases urgent immediate action is required. It is not difficult to imagine that, if this is not done, in both cases, murder could result. So, in down to earth familiar situations, Jesus is pointing out the true remedy. We cannot pride ourselves in keeping the Law or obeying God's will just because we do not kill someone else. The anger and resentment within is equally displeasing to God. That needs to be dealt with. Reconciliation, costly though it may be, is the way of true discipleship. As soon as we are conscious of a broken relationship we must take the initiative to mend it, apologize for the grievance caused, pay the debt, and make amends.

Dealing with Lust
Matthew 5: 27-30

Here again we see a similar pattern emerging. What the Teachers of the Law had done was to restrict the crime to the actual act of adultery. What Jesus does is to include thought and disposition. As with murder, the sinful action began with anger, so here the sin of adultery begins with the lustful look and imagination. It is easy to trace the progress of sin. Undisciplined sight leads to shameful imagination, and ultimately to inappropriate behaviour. It is almost an invariable rule that immoral behaviour was first entertained in the mind, and the seed was planted in the mind by what was seen. It follows, therefore, that the answer to adultery, in the followers of Jesus, includes the control of the mind and the control of the sight.

Before dealing more specifically with the remedy which Jesus identifies, we ought not to miss two important points. Firstly, even though in Jesus' teaching it is the man who looks lustfully at the woman that does not mean that it is acceptable for a woman to look lustfully at a man. Lust is essentially evil, irrespective of gender, because it treats the other as a commodity for our sexual gratification. Secondly, recognizing that we are all human, and that instincts of this kind are deeply imbedded in our humanity, we need to help each other if as Christian disciples we are to know victorious Christian living. This means that if we are serious about helping each other in the walk of discipleship we will not behave in a way, or dress in a way, which we know the other person will find titillating or provocative. It is one thing to behave and dress in a way which others find attractive, but it quite another to be deliberately seductive.

The response which Jesus makes to this issue seems brutal to say the least, so we need to remember that He is employing a common figure of speech, hyperbole, deliberately exaggerating to make the point. We see the same kind of thing in Matthew 18: 8 – 9. Then what is the point Jesus is making? If the eye is the doorway through which sin can enter your life, you need to behave as though you had lost the eye. Don't look. If your hand or foot brings temptation because of what you do or where you go, you ought to behave as though they had actually been cut off and thrown away so that you could not do those things or go to those places that cause you to sin. Christian discipline involves guarding the approach of sin. There are occasions when it is better to forego some of the experiences which this life offers in order to experience life, which is life indeed.

Dealing with Divorce
Matthew 5: 31-32

Here again, the Scribes and Pharisees were concerned with the letter of the Law. Recognizing that marriage can bring great pain as well as great joy, the Pharisees had made divorce easier to enable people to keep the Law. In fact, they had made the Law more permissive. In Jesus' culture divorce for a man was incredibly easy. All he had to do was write a certificate of divorce and give it to his wife. This could be on the grounds of her incurring his displeasure for the smallest thing. It is not difficult to imagine the way this affected society. Husbands had absolute power over their wives, and if the wife was divorced for the slightest thing she could easily find herself completely destitute.

Against this background, Jesus speaks of the institution of marriage when the Pharisees are pre-occupied with the grounds for divorce. For Jesus, divorce is a concession which is only to be allowed in the most serious cases. This is not because He is unthinking or insensitive, but because He took marriage so seriously. How easy it is, Jesus points out, for one sin to lead unavoidably to another. It is inconceivable that the kind of character described in the Beatitudes should simply write a certificate of divorce, and hand it to someone who depended upon him absolutely, resulting in the one whom he once said he loved being left helpless and destitute. Disciples don't behave like that.

Dealing with Honesty
Matthew 5: 33-37

In a vow or an oath the speaker calls upon God to witness his promise and punish him if he breaks it. The Mosaic Law laid emphasis on the evil of swearing an oath falsely (Leviticus 19: 12, Numbers 30: 2, Deuteronomy 23: 21). The Pharisees and Teachers of the Law had tried to restrict these awkward prohibitions by shifting the attention from the vow itself to the formula of words used in the vow. In effect, they were shifting the emphasis in the command from 'in vain' to 'the name of the Lord'. The consequence was that they had developed elaborate rules for making vows which made the Law less demanding. Whilst one was required to keep a vow which invoked the Divine name, one did not need to be quite so particular about vows which did not (see also Matthew 23: 16 – 22).

Against this background, what was Jesus' teaching to His disciples? Once again, He goes behind the letter of the Law and the way it had been interpreted and applied by the Teachers of the Law. Their pre-occupation with the formula was not the point of the Law at all. It did not matter whether we involved the Divine name or not, whether we swear by heaven or by earth or by Jerusalem. The disciples were not to do it. Why? Because for the followers of Jesus it is unnecessary. The standards by which they are to live include absolute honesty.

Some of us may be able to remember how in childhood, if not since, we were involved in such practices. When we wanted another person to take us really seriously we would say something like, "I swear on my mother's grave!" - whatever that means! When someone says something like this what are they really saying? They are admitting that the rest of the time they are not to be believed. Their word is not enough. To take an oath in this way is to admit one's dishonesty.

That is why the disciples of Jesus must not and need not do it. Absolute honesty for them is normal. Jesus is holding out before us a way of living in which each Christian is entirely trustworthy. We say what we mean, and we mean what we say.

Dealing with Revenge
Matthew 5: 38-42

The Mosaic Law provided a civil as well as a moral code (Exodus 21: 24, Leviticus 24: 20, Deuteronomy 19: 21). So it lays down the foundation of exact retribution, and limits compensation for those who are wronged to an exact equivalent and no more. Justice is defined, and revenge is restrained.

It may be good to pause at that point to reflect how the Mosaic Law kept the desire for revenge in check. When we are wronged by another something in us naturally wants to exact a greater penalty than the damage we have suffered. If someone has knocked one of our teeth out we like to think that he ought to lose more than one of his! So in point of fact the Mosaic Law was itself a restraint.

By the time of Jesus, the normal practice in the fulfilment of this law had moved from literal retaliation for damages to a replacement by monetary compensation. The Scribes and Pharisees, when applying this law, had also changed it, for they had moved it from the law courts, where it belonged, to the realm of personal relationships where it does not belong.

How does Jesus respond to this? For His disciples, the principle of retaliation is to be replaced by the principle of love. Jesus does not deny that the one offending is an evil person, but He does not allow His followers to retaliate. With four mini illustrations, He tells us how this principle is to be worked out in practice. We are not to allow the evil person to pull us down to their level by fostering a spirit of revenge in our hearts. Jesus' vision for His followers is that they are to be so transformed that nothing anyone does is able to stop them loving. Time and again this is echoed both in the Gospels and the Epistles. When the love of Christ fills the human heart the person loves everyone. In non-retaliation, the disciple is following his Lord.

Dealing with Opposition
Matthew 5: 43-48

If we compare verse 43 with the quote in Leviticus 19: 18 we see quite clearly what the Pharisees and Teachers of the Law had done. They had, in effect, tried to make the Law easier to keep by adding the clause "and hate your enemy". Thus, they had made the Law, not only require love, but they had made it a mandate for hatred.

Not so for the followers of Jesus. It is quite natural to love those who love us. What is exceptional and Christ-like is to love those who are our enemies, and to pray for those who persecute us. Those who collaborate with the occupying forces, as tax collectors did, and those who do not believe in God at all, the pagans, love those who love them. But we are not to be like that because Jesus was not like that. Indeed, as He points out, God the Father is not like that for He treats the good and the bad equally. They both enjoy the sunshine which God freely gives, and they both get wet when it rains! This universal Divine love, clearly seen in creation, was once and for all demonstrated in the cross of Jesus. Not only did Jesus pray for those who had nailed Him to the cross, but the very act of atoning love seen in the cross is itself evidence of

God's universal love for all, including His enemies (Romans 5:8-10).

According to the teaching of Jesus Christians are to live in a way that is quite contrary to the way people naturally live. They are to relate to one another in a way which is quite different to natural human relationships. The distinctive quality is that no matter what people do to them, they keep on loving. And Jesus' vision is not that this will be a great effort on their part, for the Law has been written on their hearts. The Spirit of an eternally loving God dwells within them, and all they are doing is living out the life that He has placed within.

It is in this context that we must understand verse 48. Perfection seems an impossible goal. How on earth can a person be perfect this side of heaven? In our own heritage it was John Wesley who reminded the whole Church of this glorious possibility. The word which is used here brings with it a distinctive understanding. It means 'fulfilling the purpose for which it was intended'; in that sense, complete, entire, and all that a loving God can make it. The radical truth which we need to grasp again is that such perfection can never be attained by our striving for it. It is not something we do. It is something which God does in us. He transforms us into the people He wants us to be.

A backward glance over the various issues which Jesus has dealt with convinces us of this truth. How is it possible never to be angry, never to look lustfully, always to be faithful, always to be absolutely honest, never to seek revenge, to love even those who are implacably opposed to all you are and all you stand for? We simply do not have what it takes to live like this. We cannot do it. But God can. He can transform who we really are on the inside so the life of discipleship is not an uphill struggle, but a day by day living out of what God has done inside.

The Disciples' Devotion
Matthew 6:1-18

A Warning
Matthew 6: 1

The kind of life which Jesus has been describing, and which He envisages for His followers is dependent on a living relationship with God. In the passage before us Jesus deals with three spiritual disciplines which would have been familiar to and expected of those who first heard this teaching – giving to the needy, prayer, and fasting. Such spiritual disciplines were in Jesus' time referred to as 'acts of righteousness'. They were expected of orthodox Jews, and clearly Jesus expects that His followers will continue these practices. Yet the distinctive thing is that when His disciples do them they will do them differently from the way they have often seen them practised.

Righteousness can all too easily become self-righteousness. We can do the right thing for the wrong reason. So subtle is human sin that our self-centredness can easily masquerade as piety. This is precisely what had happened to the religious leaders in Jesus' society. There is no suggestion that they do not give to the needy, pray, or fast. Jesus is not challenging their practice, but their motive. It is in the area of motive that His followers are to be distinctively different.

In each of these cases we have a repeating formula. It begins in each case, "When you ...". So Jesus clearly expects that His followers will do these things. Then we find Jesus highlights the contrast between the religious leaders of His day and His own disciples. It is a repeating phrase, "They have received their reward in full. But when you ..." (v2, 3, 5, 6, 16, 17). When the religious leaders make a show of their piety they undoubtedly receive the admiration of others. It is what Jesus calls 'their reward'. They give to the needy in a way that makes everyone else notice. They are admired, and the admiration is their reward. They pray in a way that is bound to make them noticed. Others admire them, and that is their reward. They fast in a way that lets everyone else know. Others admire them, and that is their reward. They have the reward of others, but that is all they have.

Jesus anticipates another reward system. It is not the reward of admiration by others. It comes from the Father. He knows what disciples do out of the public eye, and He knows why they do it. The public may not reward them, but God will.

Some Christians have a real problem with the concept of reward. It may, therefore, be helpful just to remember that Jesus is not implying that the reward which His followers receive is one stored up in heaven for them until they claim it. Jesus is not suggesting that we subject ourselves to a rigorous life of piety and devotion, making ourselves thoroughly miserable, in the hope that one day we will be rewarded in heaven. The kind of practice and motive which Jesus advocates brings its own reward here and now. The reward of giving to the needy is seeing them changed by your gift. The reward of prayer is a deeper relationship with God now. The reward of fasting now is, amongst other things, becoming master of your own appetites.

Now let us turn to reflect on each of these devotional practices in turn.

Giving to the Needy
Matthew 6: 2-4

It is clear that just as giving to the needy, sometimes called alms-giving, was regarded as an expression of Jewish faith, so it is to be with the disciples of Jesus. On reflection, it is interesting to think of how this became a feature of the first Christian communities. The poor, particularly widows and orphans, were cared for. Compassion for those in need has always been at the heart of Christian discipleship. Interestingly, when Peter and John were going to the Temple to pray they had nothing in material terms to give the beggar at the Beautiful Gate, but they still gave what they had. Self-giving love was and is a feature of Christian discipleship.

The problem was that in Jesus' community this, which should have been an expression of simple love, had become a way of expressing self-righteousness. The religious leaders did give to the needy, but they made such a show of it because their primary aim was not to meet the needs of the poor, but to receive the praise of others. Jesus calls them 'hypocrites', a word which was originally used for an orator and then an actor. It essentially describes someone who treats the world as a stage on which they perform, and assume a false identity. They want people to think they are someone or something they are not. The emphasis is on the outward show, and not on the secret places of life.

The disciples of Jesus, however, are to do things differently. When they give to the needy their aim is not the praise of others, but expressing God's love for those in need through their compassion. Because that is the aim, there is to be secrecy about what they do. It is to be secret because Jesus knew how easy it is for pride to invade the heart when others know the good things we do. This act of compassion is to be so secret that no one else knows. Using a powerful figure of speech, Jesus recognizes that normally the right hand is the active one with which a gift would be handed over, but in His disciples the act is to be so secret that even the left hand does not know what is going on. This is because self-consciousness can all too easily become self-righteousness.

Even though others are unaware of the disciple's kindness, and even though the kindness is done without any self-consciousness, God knows, and the Father will reward the disciple in His own way.

Prayer
Matthew 6: 5-15

Clearly it is the expectation of Jesus that just as prayer was a spiritual discipline for Jewish people, so it would continue to be for His followers. Yet once again He identifies the error in the way this discipline was often practised. Those whom Jesus called 'hypocrites' did in fact love to pray, but the reason for their prayer was entirely wrong. It was not expressing love or praise for the God to whom they were supposedly praying. Rather, it was used as an opportunity to parade themselves and their righteousness. It is this wrong motive that Jesus is criticizing. They already have their reward in the admiration of other people, but that is all they have. Their ulterior motive in making prayer an exhibitionist display destroys it as an authentic act.

Jesus' disciples are to pray in a different way. They should close the door against the prying eyes of others, and the disturbances and distractions of the world. There, in the secret place, they will encounter the Father. Nothing enriches the life of prayer like a sense of a personal encounter with God. The result is an ever deeper relationship with Him. How interesting it is that in these verses the 'you' is in the singular. Prayer is about a personal encounter and a personal relationship with God.

Exhibitionism is not the only sin to be avoided in prayer. Vain repetition is also identified. The word 'babbling' seems to suggest, not only vain repetition, but meaningless, mechanical repetition and speech with the associated mistaken belief that the more they say the more they will be heard. The disciple is not to be like this, for such a practice is based on a mistaken idea about God. God is not ignorant, and so He does not need to hear from us; nor is He reluctant, so we do not need to persuade Him.

The prayer which Jesus gave His disciples as a model for their own recognizes the holiness, love, care, and willingness of

God, our needs, our responsibilities, and God's power. Much has been written about it which need not be repeated here, save to say what a tragedy it would be if the prayer which Jesus gave us as the perfect model for the prayer of His followers should become the vain repetitious babbling which He so condemned.

At its heart Christian prayer, as Jesus understood it, is God-centred and not self-centred, and is intelligent and not mindless.

Fasting
Matthew 6: 16-18

There is little doubt that most disciples today recognise their responsibility in giving to the needy and prayer. Jesus clearly understands that His disciples will also fast. This was a familiar Jewish devotional practice. We see it mentioned many times in the Old Testament: on occasions of national penitence (Judges 20: 26, 1 Samuel 7: 6), as a way of preparing for a specific revelation (Daniel 9: 3), and as a way of humbling oneself before God in penitence (Psalm 35: 13, Isaiah 58: 3, 5).

Fasting, as here understood, is for a period, and as a spiritual discipline, depriving oneself of something enjoyed, usually food. As a spiritual discipline it did not always go with prayer, but often was linked with prayer when individuals or communities needed to seek the guidance or blessing of God on some particular issue (2 Chronicles 20: 1ff). Throughout Christian history, fasting has been recognised as a discipline with a number of virtues. It expresses our solidarity with the poor and hungry. It demonstrates to God how serious we are about the life of discipleship; it keeps things in proportion, and clearly indicates who is the master. Do we control our appetites, or do our appetites control us? Many Christians in our own generation are rediscovering the value of fasting, especially in a world of such extremes of both hunger and obesity.

As with giving to the needy and prayer, the criticism of Jesus is that what is essentially a personal matter had been made into a public affair. The Scribes and Teachers of the Law in Jesus' generation would fast twice a week on Mondays and Thursdays. It just happened that these were market days, so more people were around to notice how righteous they were! They went out of their way to have their righteousness noted by others, and they had their reward.

In contrast, the followers of Jesus are to take pains to disguise their fasting. Its purpose was not to advertise them or their devotion, but as a personal discipline. They were to wash and brush up as usual so that it was not obvious to others. According to the teaching of Jesus, fasting was not to gain a spiritual reputation, but to demonstrate our humility before God alone. To do that, to recognise again our true position in relation to God, is reward enough.

In dealing with these spiritual disciplines, Jesus has placed before us two alternatives: hypocrisy or reality. The effect of hypocritical behaviour in the devotional life is that it destroys our integrity. It is driven by our pride. In these and all spiritual matters the true disciple needs always to remember who he is doing it for; not the admiration of others, not the pride of self, but out of love and devotion to God.

The Disciples' Choices
Matthew 6: 19-24

Already in our studies we have seen that the Sermon on the Mount is fiercely counter-cultural. The way the disciple lives is to be different from those around him. This is because he is motivated and driven by different things. His deep, personal, inward desires are different from other people's and they touch and change all that his is and does.

In the previous section Jesus has contrasted different areas of the disciple's life. There is the private, secret place, and there is the public display. There are the religious and devotional practices, and there is the way we live in the secular world. In contrasting the life of the disciple with the lives of the teachers of the law Jesus has made it plain that God is equally concerned for every area of our lives. We cannot excuse ourselves by claiming that one area is concerning our religious life and another is not. The life of a disciple will not be lived in compartments like that. It will be lived in such a way that there will be no part of it which cannot, in good conscience, be offered to God.

But, of course, the way we live is to a large extent determined by the people we are. Behaviour follows character. But how is character to be shaped? It is to this question that Jesus now turns. His answer is that our character is shaped by the things we value. If we cherish something, the desire which we have for it will change both the way we think and our subsequent behaviour. So it is that Jesus focuses on four different issues and identifies the choices we have to make if we are to discover the wonder of true discipleship.

Two Treasures
Matthew 6: 19-21

The first choice which Jesus identifies concerns two possible treasures which people can possess, or more correctly the location in which these treasures are held. There is treasure on earth and treasure in heaven. The implication is that they are mutually exclusive. We all wish it were not so, but it is. We cannot have treasures both on earth and in heaven.

This is extremely challenging for us all in an acquisitive, materialistic society; so it is very important to identify what Jesus is not saying. He is not prohibiting possessions *per se*, nor is He condemning the prudence which leads us to put something by 'for a rainy day'. His disciples, like the rest of humankind, are expected to enjoy the good gifts of our Creator, graciously provided for His children. Rather, it is the selfishness of possessing which is condemned. We need to remember the emphasis which Jesus placed on 'for yourselves' and the word 'treasure'. He is condemning the selfish attitude which simply seeks to acquire more and more things when they are not needed, the kind of extravagant living which places self at the centre of the picture, and is indifferent to the needs of the poor, the covetousness which is unable to rest whilst others have what you want, even though you have no idea what you would do with it if you had it!

The stark contrast which Jesus lays before us convinces us of the sheer common sense of His teaching. What is the point of amassing more and more possessions when, by the very order of things, they are so vulnerable, prone to rust, decay, vermin and theft? How much more sensible it is to establish our store where these things are no longer a threat, and where we can be sure that our treasure will be safe.

In the ancient world nothing was safe. People went to extraordinary lengths to secure their property. Yet their efforts pale into insignificance compared with our own. We have developed insecticides, rust proof paint and sophisticated burglar alarms. Yet with all that we can do to protect what we own we are all very vulnerable. The constant threat of inflation, an economic slump, or simply the progress of technology can wipe out the value of our possessions at a stroke. And even if we manage to avoid all these things and we retain our possessions throughout our whole lives, there comes a time when we will have to leave it all behind. There is something very sad about someone who has spent the whole of life gaining wealth, building a business, becoming part of the social set, and then when life is ebbing away they make the discovery that all that they have is going to be of no use whatsoever when death has closed the door behind them.

But it need not be like that, and it will not be like that for the disciple of Jesus, for the disciple will have learned the things which really matter. These things will be the wealth which he possesses. The world may jeer, or stand back in silent admiration. His value systems will not be understood. Some may even pity him, but when it really matters he will have what it takes.

Jesus does not explain what the treasures in heaven really are. But bearing in mind the contrast which he identifies between the transient, vulnerable nature of things here and the permanent, safe nature of things there one can take it that he is speaking of things which will be of significance in eternity. It is very challenging to enquire of the eternal worth of so much that we do. What effect will what we do have in eternity? Will it matter then?

Whilst much of our time is spent doing things which will be of no value then, many of our activities, temporal though they are, can have eternal consequences. Paul tells us that faith, hope and love abide. If we can help another to grow in their knowledge of Christ, if we can use our resources to express the compassion of Christ, if we can give ourselves to build a world which honours Christ, if we can lead another to Christ, these are the things which will last for ever. No burglar can steal these; no moth eat them, nor will they rust away. They last for ever. These are the things which the disciple will live for. In fact, they will become his treasure.

Two Ways of Seeing
Matthew 6: 22-23

Conscious as we are of the need to live out authentic discipleship in God's world we are confronted with another question. How do we wean ourselves away from a love for the world, and cultivate a love for heavenly treasure? Jesus offers us two answers in v 22-24. The first concerns the way we see things, and the second concerns what we serve.

In the first we are presented with two contrasting conditions: the sighted person and the blind person. Speaking metaphorically, Jesus says that the eye is the lamp of the body. It is important to notice that he does not speak of the eye as a window which lets light in, but rather a lamp which gives light. The consequent emphasis, therefore, is that the eye and the sight it gives, enables the whole body to do other things more effectively and more efficiently; just as we can do all sorts of things if we can see what we are doing because we have a lamp in a dark place. The eye enables other things because the eye enables sight. Even though it may be daylight all around, the blind person walks in darkness, and the sighted person walks in light, simply because the eye enables him to do so.

Further, we would do well to remember the number of occasions in scripture when the eye and the sight it enables is used to describe ambition. We speak of fixing our eye on something when we make it central to the task in hand. Just as the eye affects our whole body, so our ambition affects our whole life. Just as a seeing eye gives light to the whole body, so a single-minded ambition to serve God throws light on all we do. If our overwhelming desire is to serve the Lord it will touch everything we do. Conversely, blindness plunges the whole body into darkness and so ambition becomes selfish; exactly the condition Jesus has spoken of in the previous passage, laying up treasures on earth. How easy it is to live for this world alone. Why do people do it? Because they have never seen as the disciple has seen. Why have they not seen? Because their eyes are bad. The whole body is in darkness. Yet how wonderful when the Holy Spirit comes and enables us to see things as we have never seen before. That changes everything. By the grace of God the blind can see and everything is different.

Two Masters
Matthew 6: 24

Once again there is a contrast. There are two possible masters for every life, and there are two ways of relating to them. Jesus makes it plain as plain as can be. The disciple cannot serve two masters. It is impossible. There are many today who try very hard to do so. Some will try to apportion their time, some for God and some for themselves. Some will try to apportion their wealth, give God some and do what we want with the rest. Jesus already has identified some of the ways which his contemporaries tried; serving God with the lips and themselves with the heart, serving God in appearances and serving self in reality. Whatever system we may adopt it is doomed to fail, because Jesus said it is impossible.

In order to appreciate the strength of Jesus' teaching we need to focus on the word 'Master'. It is taken from a culture in which servant-hood and even slavery were common. There it was simply impossible to serve two masters. The servant was absolutely committed to the master, to do his bidding, every moment. The slave was actually owned by the master who could do with him exactly as he wished. The message is clear. Jesus is speaking of single ownership and full-time service.

The two masters who compete for allegiance are identified as God and money. They are so diametrically opposed to one another that it is impossible to serve both. If you attempt to divide your loyalty you have already given in to money because God can only be served with an entire and exclusive devotion. The word here translated 'money' was 'mammon' in the Authorised Version. It comes from an ancient Aramaic word meaning 'wealth'. There is the contrast. It is impossible to be devoted to both God and wealth. You either love one and hate the other or are devoted to one and despise the other. That is the choice.

We would do well to remember that, hard as this teaching is, Jesus is speaking of serving and not using. He does not condemn using money or wealth. Indeed, he spoke of using money more than once, making donations in the temple and paying taxes. Christians do live in the world where money and wealth are our currency. Jesus was not advocating here a strict renunciation of such a society. Rather the emphasis lies on what we serve.

It was the puritan, Thomas Goodwin, who helpfully reminded his people of the contrast between what we use and what is our master. The disciple may use money and wealth, but they are not his master. In the same way, those who are not disciples may use God or the church, but they are not his master either. The challenge concerns what we really serve and what we allow to become our master. And we all know how subtle sin is, how easy it is to begin by being in control, and then gradually, and insidiously things change. We began by being in control. Before long what we were controlling begins to control us. We like to think that we are strong enough to remain in charge. We are not. Only God can master the human heart. That is why the disciple is one who exclusively and entirely devotes himself to God. He keeps a loose hold on the world, enjoying what God gives, but always recognizing the dangers. After all, wealth is man-made, so to serve it is idolatry.

This teaching raises profound questions concerning, not only the personal conduct of individual disciples, but the shape of society, since so much of our political system is driven by wealth creation. It is in just such a world that the Christian should stand out as belonging to another kingdom where the things of this world count for nothing, but things eternal count for everything.

The Disciples' Peace
Matthew 6: 25-34

It is the clear intention of Jesus that his disciples should be set free from the tensions, stresses and strains which others know. As we establish a new and proper relationship with the things of this world, as we begin to see things clearly, and get a new vision to motivate our ambition, as we remain in control, by the grace of God, of the things which so easily can control us; so we are set free from so many of the things which trouble and worry those who live around us.

The 'therefore' with which this passage begins makes us look back to what has gone before. Of the two treasures, of the two ways of seeing, and of the two masters, which does common sense determine that you choose? Here we are called to live out our sensible choices and know the impact which that has on our whole life.

Yet we know all too well that most of us live at two levels: the intellectual and the emotional. We can know something, but at an emotional level we are still troubled. It is precisely this trouble which Jesus wants us to be liberated from. Once again we have a contrast. It is the choice between being anxious about our body on the one hand and seeking God's kingdom and His righteousness first of all on the other. It is about what we are seeking. It is characteristic of pagans that their lives are overshadowed by concerns of the material world. For the disciple, things are to be different.

How interesting that Jesus identifies three areas of particular concern – food, drink and clothes. If this was a feature of Jesus' society it is certainly a feature of our own. The media, our culture, and our contemporaries in the secular world all point us to the overwhelming concerns which most people are expected to have concerning the welfare of the body. Think of the number of advertisements and television programmes devoted to food, drink and clothing. Think of the importance which image has to many, and how it often determines whether one is accepted in a social class or group. How pertinent, therefore, is the teaching of Jesus for today.

Let's be clear about the heart of Jesus' teaching here. To be engrossed on material comforts, Jesus says, is a false and shallow preoccupation. His disciples are to make a stand against it. It is unproductive, for we cannot add an hour to our lives by worrying about it (v27). It is unnecessary because our Heavenly Father knows what we need (v32). It is unworthy of his disciples because it gives the impression that your real worth is determined by what you eat, drink and wear (v25). The true disciple knows that life is of much more significance than this.

To help us grasp the point Jesus uses illustrations which are commonplace. He speaks of birds and flowers. We have much to learn from them. Clearly the birds are expected to forage for food, and in that sense at least co-operate with God. They do not worry, but they do not sit back and wait for it to be delivered either. The flowers of the field excel in beauty by being what God has made them to be. In both cases they find that their purpose in fulfilled, not by anxious stress, but by resting in God's order, design and provision.

He then presents the clear logic by arguing from the lesser to the greater. Paul does the same kind of thing at the end of Romans 8. Here Jesus is affirming two undeniable facts. God provides for the birds of the air and flowers of the field. They, by being what they were made to be, recognize their dependence on Him. And secondly, people are more important in God's eyes than birds and flowers. It is inconceivable that God should consider lilies more important than people. The consequence which Jesus draws, therefore, is undeniable. If God cares for them, we can count on Him to care for us.

Of course, this does not set us free from the responsibility of working for our living, no more than the birds can sit back and wait for food to be delivered. Nor does it mean that we can ignore the poor and needy as though God will look after them as He wills. In a needy world like ours the essential problem is not divine provision but human distribution. For so few of the world's population to hold so much of its resources is simply iniquitous. The disciple, who really belongs to another world, inspired by a vision of God's kingdom will be committed to a just society where provision is fairly distributed. Nor does Jesus suggest that the disciple can expect to be free from trouble. He did not teach it. In fact he clearly teaches the opposite. Each day has enough trouble (v34). History has proved the point. But to be free from trouble and to be free from worry are not the same thing. Many of the greatest saints who have gone before us have not been free from trouble, but in the hard place they have found a way of trusting their Father and of knowing His gracious provision for all their needs.

So, once again, we are faced with two alternatives. On the one hand we can live like pagans whose lives are dominated by concerns about their food, drink and clothing – and all the image building and class consciousness which follow. On the other hand the disciple of Jesus lives by another standard. The command is to seek God's kingdom first. The disciple will bend all his energies to seeking and establishing the rule and reign of God. He will constantly be asking what life would be like if Jesus was Lord there, and he will give everything he has and is to that great end.

He will also seek God's righteousness. The kingdom is where God's reign is acknowledged. His righteousness concerns the standards of His kingdom spilling over into the world. The world may not know him yet, but the disciple will seek the righteousness of God everywhere. How will he do it? In a variety of ways, but principally by living in a way which makes righteousness attractive. He will be the kind of person who moves through life and makes others long for what he has discovered. In the end the question is not whether our hopes, dreams and ambitions are small or large, but whom they are for. To live as part of God's kingdom, according to the teaching of Christ is to set our hearts free from the worry that bedevils so many. To discover that peace, to rest in God's gracious provision, to be content in whatever circumstances we find ourselves; this is the calling of the disciple, and who in their right mind would not want to be part of a kingdom like that?

The Disciples' Relationships
Matthew 7: 1-12

As we move into the next major section of the Sermon on the Mount it is not difficult to recognize that relationships are the common theme. There are the relationships with fellow disciples, those whom Jesus calls 'your brother', a new kind of relationship with the Heavenly Father, and our relationships in evangelism.

Looking back on the journey we have travelled so far through this amazing teaching we see that Jesus has dealt with the disciples' attitude, influence, goodness, devotion, and ambition. The very fact that He now moves on to speak about relationships indicates his awareness of the challenge that this area would present to those who would follow Him. From our own experience too, we recognize how difficult honest, open, true and loving relationships are. As the gospel story unfolds we see that even amongst that small group of the first disciples, their relationships with each other, and with others proved to be a problem. If we think they were a happy band of pilgrims who always got on well with each other and were welcomed by all they met, we fool ourselves. The gospel evidence is that there was rivalry amongst them, even in the shadow of the cross. They sought to prevent those coming to Jesus whom he would welcome, namely children. And when we consider their relationship with the world we see that they misunderstood who were their enemies and who were their friends, and in their over-enthusiasm sought to invoke the judgment of God on those who did not readily accept their teaching.

It ought not to be a surprise to us, therefore, when we realize that relationships are still a challenge today. In our own generation, when churches are sometimes wrecked by relationships which have gone sour, where some Christians refuse to have fellowship with other Christians purely because they see things differently, where our idea of the nature and character of God is sometimes a long way from that of Jesus, where the world presses in on every side and where there are those, sometimes with large followings, whose motives are maybe not the best; we shall see how pertinent this teaching is, not just for the first disciples, but for those in every generation who would follow Him.

With other Disciples
Matthew 7: 1-5

How are those who would be disciples of Jesus to relate to others who would also be disciples of Jesus? This is the issue here addressed.   Our understanding is that this applies, of course, in the local church; but it also bridges the denominational divide.   Jesus is referring to relationships between all who would follow him, irrespective of their denominational allegiance. His teaching is very clear.

First of all, Jesus says, a Christian is not to be a judge (v1-2). Clearly this does not mean that the legal profession is closed to him; since Jesus is speaking about relationships between Christians, and not the Christian's choice of career or his attitude to secular legislative authority; nor can it mean that we must never make any judgments about other people at all. That would make life impossible, and would also make it impossible to fulfil the injunction of v6, since there we are required to judge who are dogs and who are pigs!

Jesus is condemning an attitude of censoriousness amongst his followers. That is always wrong. Why? Because it is built on the understanding that the other person must conform to your standards, image and requirements.   They are not your servants and you are not their master. They do not have to live according to your standard. They are not answerable to you, but to Him.

We are all products of our past and as such we all have a mental picture of what a Christian ought to be like. In many cases it is bred into us. We believe that some things are acceptable and others are not. But if we think about it closely we often discover that many of these things have nothing whatsoever to do with being a Christian. They often concern matters of dress and behaviour, especially in church. We think we know what a real Christian ought to look like, dress like, behave like; and when we encounter others who do not conform to our ideals we give the impression that they do not fit and are not acceptable. Often Christians are the worst offenders in this regard. There are many outside the church today who would be inside if they had not been made to feel unwelcome because they did not conform to the required image.

Of course, if we set ourselves up as the judges of other Christians we must remember that we will be judged in the same way. We can claim no ignorance of a law that we take it upon ourselves to administer. What a challenge this is, especially when we remember that most of us fail to live up to our own ideals, let alone those of others. Humility before God is required of us all. Jesus is not asking that his disciples are so blind to the faults of those around them that they cannot help them on the journey, but he is making a plea for generosity; one which we need to hear as clearly today as ever.

Secondly, a Christian is not to be a hypocrite (v3-4). Of course, this is a joke. It is one example of the wit of Jesus. He is painting a caricature of the situation. Like a cartoonist, he is exaggerating the feature he wishes to emphasize. How can a man have a plank in his eye? It is ridiculous. Yet it does highlight a fatal tendency in us all. We tend to exaggerate the faults of others whilst being blind to our own faults. We can see the failings of others so clearly, but we never see our own. Now Jesus is very clear. The disciple will be one who will constantly be applying his critical faculty to himself rather than, and certainly before, he applies it to other Christians. This is because he will be someone who recognizes his obligation to live in a way that is pleasing to his master. Far from being someone who is always pointing the finger at others in a disapproving way, the disciple will be someone who is living in an attitude of self-examination, and seeking to bring his life into conformity with the divine will.

How is this to be achieved? We all need help, and Jesus recognized that. His picture of the disciples journeying together is not one of a company where they are always criticizing each other. Instead they will, each one, be seeking to deal with the faults that they discover in their own lives and, with the benefit of this experience they will be able to help each other as they travel together.

Relationships in Evangelism
Matthew 7:6

In order to get to the heart of Jesus' teaching here we need to discover how both dogs and pigs were seen in Jesus' society. Far from being the family pet that dogs have become in more recent years, in Jesus' generation they were scavengers. Like vermin they fed on what they could find. To the Jew, of course, pigs were unclean animals, held in contempt by every religious person. So here Jesus is using a metaphor. He speaks of dogs and pigs as those who have no regard for the clean or the holy. They represent those whom the disciples will encounter who have absolutely no regard for what is either precious or sacred.

What happens if precious and sacred things are given to dogs and pigs? They are trampled underfoot. The true nature of the offering is totally disregarded. Now this, Jesus says, is a situation which the disciple will encounter as he shares the good news. There will be those whom he will encounter who, because of their very nature, have no regard for the precious nature of the gospel, the holiness of God, or indeed any awareness of the spiritual dimension of life. What will be their response if the precious truth of the gospel is shared with them? It will be totally disregarded. They simply do not have it in themselves to recognize the true nature of that which is being offered to them. We ought not to be surprised when the message, precious though it is, is rejected.

This teaching is essentially about a strategy for effective evangelism. To offer the gospel to all, expecting all to respond positively to the message, is simply inappropriate. If the message is to be understood for what it really is, and if it is to receive a positive response, something first needs to happen in the hearts of those to whom it is offered. Their spirit needs to be awakened to the things of God. That is why prayer and evangelism go together. In order to share effectively the good news something first needs to happen in the hearer. But we cannot do it. It is the Holy Spirit's ministry. He is able to quicken within the hearts of those outside the kingdom an awareness of the things of God, indeed a hunger for them. When this has happened the message will be met in a quite different way. There will be a welcome and ready acceptance. How is it to happen? God will meet the need as we come to him in pleading prayer. It is no accident, therefore, that Jesus now moves on to deal with this very matter.

A New Relationship with God
Matthew 7: 7-12

It is no accident that this passage stands at the heart of this section dealing with relationships. It is the fulcrum on which everything else turns. If we are to have the kind of relationships with others required by v1-6, if we are to have the discernment required by v7, and indeed by v 13-23, then we need a living relationship with God as our heavenly Father. This relationship is expressed, amongst other things, through prayer. It is to this that our Lord now turns.

He is addressing his disciples, and He makes the amazing promise that if they ask, it will be given, if they seek they will find, and if they knock it will be opened to them. Some have seen in these three dimensions of prayer an ascending scale of intensity. One begins by asking; one goes on seeking. If that does not produce an answer one knocks repeatedly with increasing loudness. Others have drawn a parallel with a child looking for a parent because they want something. If the parent is close at hand they ask. If they do not know where the parent is they seek. And if the parent seems to be inaccessible because they are away, say in their room, the child knocks. However we understand this teaching we cannot miss the amazing nature of the promise. Asking results in receiving; seeking in finding; and knocking in the door being opened. Removing the barrier results in a relationship which can be freely expressed, without any hindrance.

Further, how interesting it is to identify those to whom Jesus makes the promise. When speaking of asking, seeking and knocking he is addressing disciples. But as he affirms the promise it is 'everyone'. His rationale is to move from the general to the particular. It is in the nature of God to react in this way to everyone, so the disciples can be confident when they come before One with whom they have a special and distinctive relationship.

In order to reinforce the truth Jesus gives a short parable, a word picture of the disciple's relationship with God. The message is plain to see. If we who are intrinsically evil and selfish, will respond lovingly to the requests of our children, how much more will God, who is intrinsically good, respond positively to us when we ask, seek and knock. The father in the story will not give the stone or snake because he loves his child. To do so would be unthinkable. Indeed, it would force us to re-think our understanding of the father's relationship with his child. The nature of the gift depends on the nature of the relationship and fundamentally on the disposition of the father's heart toward his child.

Once we have come to recognize God as our loving Father, Jesus says, we can count on his loving and positive response to our prayers. His response is determined not by something in us but by something in Him, namely his overwhelming love for all His children. It was in his teaching on prayer earlier in the Sermon on the Mount that Jesus invited his disciples to call God their Father, just as He did. It was a revolution in their thinking. We miss its impact because we have become so familiar with this terminology. So it's worth reminding ourselves that Jerimaias, a great New Testament scholar searched all the prayer literature in ancient Judaism in search of the word 'Abba' as a name for God. He was unable to find a single reference. Here is something entirely new. It is on the nature of this new relationship that the life of prayer depends, for prayer both expresses that relationship and depends upon it.

Once we have grasped this father/child relationship as Jesus meant it to be understood we find that so many of our supposed difficulties with prayer are dealt with. Granted there are an increasing number in our society who does not have a good father role model on which they can base their theological understanding, yet the truth as Jesus shared it still remains true. The best picture we can have of the relationship which Jesus means us to have with God is the relationship of which the father/child is an earthly reflection. Some may not have known a good father, but through becoming a disciple of Jesus they can discover that God can become the Father that they have never known but always longed for.

If the relationship between the father and son is a close one the father will often know what the child wants before the child asks. So it is with God. He knows everything. The purpose of prayer is not to tell God of our wants, or to remind Him, as though He had forgotten. Yet the earthly father will wait for the child to express his desire, not because he is thereby informing the father but because it is appropriate for the child to express his needs to a father in whose love he can be confident. The child who gets everything he wants without even taking the trouble to ask usually finishes up as a spoilt brat. God is too loving to want that for any of His children.
Furthermore, any earthly father knows that for the child just to ask is not enough. Deep desires need to be evidenced by sustained requests. It is not because the father is unwilling to

give. After all he loves the child. But he does want the child to grow to maturity understanding that things that are to be valued do not come easily. They cannot be given in response to some whim or because it happens to be the latest craze. Sometimes over a sustained period of time the child has to make the request known before he receives the gift. He is not wearing down the father's resistance, because the father is not resistant anyway, but he is demonstrating that here is something that he really, really wants, and he is serious about sustaining his request. The consequence is that when the gift is eventually received it is valued far more highly than it would have been if it had been given straight away.

Yet we all know that sometimes with all the persistence in prayer that we can muster our prayers still seem to go unanswered, or at least we do not get what we desire. How are we to square that with the teaching of Jesus here? Maybe it forces us to think again about the whole subject of prayer. Maybe we have fundamentally misunderstood what prayer is really all about. Certainly prayer is not a kind of Aladdin's lamp which we rub to get God to do what we want!

We return to where we began this section. Prayer is fundamentally about a relationship with God. It is the chief way in which that relationship is expressed and one of the most significant ways that it grows. The plain fact is that if God is all-loving, as He is, and if His knowledge of me and my past, present and future is all-encompassing; then there are some times when God has to say, "My dear child, despite all your pleading, I cannot give you what you request. It is not because I do not love you that I am doing this, but precisely because I love you so much." We need to remember that we are following One who, one dark night in a garden, asked, sought and knocked. But the Father had to say, "No. My Son I cannot take this cup away from you. What you ask is simply not possible. My love forbids it." It was the late Rev Dr Martin Lloyd-Jones who once wrote, "I am profoundly grateful to God that he did not grant me certain things for which I asked, and that He shut certain doors in my face." There are many, with the benefit of hindsight, who could echo those words.

It is, of course, no accident that this teaching, focusing on our relationship with God expressed in the life of prayer, leads to what many have described as the 'Golden Rule' in v 12. Jesus is advocating such a maturity in our faith, such an intimate trust in God, that we are content to leave our destiny and desires in His almighty, loving hands. The child must understand that all requests cannot be immediately granted. Yet the motive for delay or refusal lies in the unquestionable love of the father. We, therefore, may sometimes need to act in a similar way to others. There are times when what we do will be immediately recognizable as a loving response. But there are other times when it may appear unloving, even though it is not, just as God's response to our pleading sometimes appears. We behave in a loving way towards others, because that is how God responds to us and that is how we want others to respond to us. But we recognize that this does not mean that we immediately give them whatever they want. Indeed, this may prove to be the most unloving thing we could do. We also recognize that is how others ought to behave toward us. To really love the other person is not a sentimental thing; it is always to seek their greater good. Whilst often that means saying 'yes', sometimes it may mean saying 'no'.

The Disciples' Decision
Matthew 7: 13-29

As the Sermon on the Mount nears its climax we cannot fail to notice that we are all confronted with a choice. It is the challenge to true discipleship. Throughout the sermon Jesus has been speaking of two ways of approaching life. There were two kinds of goodness, two kinds of devotion, two treasures, two masters, and two ambitions. Now he seeks to confront all those who would be His disciples with the inevitable decision which they have to make. His teaching demands that we make a choice. Like any good preacher, Jesus hammers this home with a number of successive blows.

He confronts the first hearers, and us, with examples of this all important choice which we have to make. There are two ways along which we can travel, two kinds of teachers whom we can follow, two kinds of response we can make, and two kinds of foundations on which we can build.

This choice between two options makes us uncomfortable. We wish there were more. We would prefer at least three, and most would prefer an unlimited number, so large in fact that we could simply do our own thing, live our own way and still claim to be His disciples. It is not so. We all have to choose.

Two Ways
Matthew 7: 13-14

The contrast between the two ways could not have been greater. One is easy and broad, and many take it. The other is hard and narrow and few find it. We know that the way ahead for a true disciple will be both challenging and unpopular. If we want to travel with the crowd and have an easy walk, the broad way will be the one we choose.

There are also two ways into these two ways. One is very wide and easy. The implication is that anyone can get through such a gate. In fact, the gate is so wide that you can take lots of things through with you. But the other entrance is different. It is hard to find, suggesting that any who take it have had to search for it. It could easily have been missed in the bustle of life. The entrance to this way is narrow, like a turnstile at a football match or the gate in an airport departure lounge. It is not built to accommodate us and all our baggage. In fact it is so narrow that we have to enter this gate one at a time and in order to get through the gate we have to leave most of the baggage behind.

There are two destinations, for both these roads lead somewhere. The wide gate opens on to a broad way: broad enough to accommodate the great crowds who travel that road. Yet the destination of that way is destruction, with the chill which such a thought brings to the soul. There is an awful sadness about those who have gone in at an easy gate, travelled a broad road with great crowds, without every thinking where the road leads. On the other hand, the narrow gate opens to a narrow way. The traveller will never be part of the crowd. Popularity is not to be found here. The journey will be hard. It will call for all the strength that the traveller can muster. But the destination is life, with the thrill which such a thought brings to the soul. Like a mountain climber surveying the landscape from the summit after a hard climb, this traveller will know that the destination has made the journey worth it.

These two ways are before us all. Everyone who has heard or has read the Sermon on the Mount can see the option before them. The inevitable choice has to be made.

Two Kinds of Teachers
Matthew 7: 15-20

Those who would be disciples, not only have to choose between two roads before them, but they also have to choose between two kinds of teachers who would persuade them.

There are, of course, assumptions which lie behind this teaching. The first is the uncomfortable fact that there have been, there are, and probably there always will be, false prophets: those who do not teach the truth. Within the pages of the New Testament we see various examples of those whom Paul encountered during his ministry. In the various letters he writes fiercely against them. They might have been very nice people. Certainly they spoke in a persuasive way. They were probably quite good preachers. But the content of their message was not based on truth but on falsehood.

The second assumption which lies behind this passage is that there is an objective standard of truth from which one can depart; teach others the error and so become a false prophet. The idea of objective truth has become less and less popular in our generation. We like to feel that everyone can believe whatever they choose and as long as they are reasonably good, pleasant people they will be alright in the end. The Bible knows nothing of such a view. Truth matters. The gospel cannot mean whatever you choose it should mean. The disciple of Jesus will be one who recognizes this and resists the temptation to follow the false prophet, however popular he may be.

The warning of Jesus is plain. We are to watch out for the false prophet. Be on your guard. Just because someone says something which appears attractive, it does not mean that it is true. Sift and weigh what you hear. Judge everything according to the standard set out in scripture and affirmed by the teaching of the church over twenty centuries.

We must also be aware of their motives. They are not pure or honouring to the Lord. Every shepherd in Jesus' generation knew what havoc a wolf could wreak amongst a flock of sheep. The idea of a wolf dressed in a sheepskin so it will not be recognized is frightening indeed. But so is the idea of the persuasive preacher, feigning piety, using orthodox language but meaning something quite different by it. No wonder we are to be on our guard.

Of course, this begs the question of how you distinguish between the true and the false. Jesus makes the answer plain. To do so he changes the metaphor from sheep and wolves to tree and fruit. You know the tree by its fruit. You know the spurious as well as the authentic by their fruit. What is the fruit? It is both character and conduct. To put it bluntly; how does this person's life and character square up with the teaching of the Sermon on the Mount which we have studied so far? Are they walking with their Lord in purity and holiness? Are they in love with the world or in love with the Saviour? Is their ambition driven by selfishness or the glory of God? For

J.C Ryle was right in affirming that sound doctrine and holy living were the unmistakable fruit of the true Christian teacher.

This teaching is challenging indeed, so maybe a word of caution ought to be added. The Lord is not honoured by witch-hunts. It is not the intention of the Saviour that we should all spend most of our time trying to work out whether the other person is 'sound'. Indeed, such an attitude contradicts the teaching we have already studied in the Sermon on the Mount. Whilst we are to be on our guard against false teachers we must not confuse heresy with immaturity. If we might be allowed to push Jesus' metaphor, fruit needs time to ripen. Do not write someone off when their only crime is that they have not been a Christian as long as you. Nor should we take the reports of others on face value. Sometimes they will have their own agendas. If you think there is a wolf in sheep's clothing you need to get pretty close to do a detailed examination.

Yet having said it all, the choice is before us once again. This time it is the choice between truth and falsehood. Yet again it cannot be avoided.

Two Responses
Matthew 7: 21-23

How significant it is that Jesus follows the warning we have just considered with the passage to which we now turn. Doctrine matters, but doctrine alone is not enough. There will be those who both on this day and on that day will make the correct doctrinal affirmation, but they will not enter the kingdom of heaven.

Let's be clear about the two responses that Jesus outlines. On the one hand, there are those who will say the right things. They use the right language. In fact, they not only use the right language but they had an apparently effective ministry. When they claim that they have prophesied, driven out demons and performed miracles the Lord does not contradict them. Yet even all that is not enough. On the other hand there are those whom Jesus describes by saying that they do the will of His father who is in heaven. That is to say, the profession which they make with their lips is so profound, authentic and genuine that it touches every area of their lives. Because Jesus is their Lord their overwhelming concern is to do the will of the Father. They may, or may not, have prophesied, driven out demons and performed miracles. The verbal profession, or the extraordinary manifestation is not what gains admission to the kingdom of heaven, but only doing the Father's will.

The choice before the would-be disciple is the choice between the easy option of saying the right things and having what appears to be an effective ministry on the one hand, and on the other living a life of surrender to the will of God. Once the commitment is complete and the heart yielded to God's will everything falls into place. Yet without this everything is, at best, a sham.

We must not underestimate the verbal profession which was made. It was orthodox, and repeated with enthusiasm. It was not made in a private place where no one else could see, but publicly and in spectacular fashion. Yet it was unacceptable, as was the ministry which followed from it, because it did not spring from a yielded heart.

How challenging this is for us all. How easy it is to think that just because we say the right things to the right people in the right places we are alright. How easy it is to believe that just because others recognize the effectiveness of our ministry all is well. How it cuts to the heart to learn that the final test concerns not what we say, or what we do, but who we are. The choice, from which once again we cannot hide, is whether we are to yield the will, that last bastion of self, to the Master we seek to serve. That is what makes the difference now and that is what will make the difference then.

Two Foundations
Matthew 7: 24-27

As we move to this final section and this familiar parable we recognize a subtle change in the challenge. In the former passage the contrast was between saying and doing. There were those who said the right things but did not do the will of God. Here the contrast is between hearing and doing. The danger is that we will all hear, but only some will allow that teaching to have such an impact upon them that it will change what they do.

The difference between the two buildings in the parable was not in their appearance, but their foundation. In may be that both were equally admired by the passer-by. But only one stood the test when the storm came. The most important thing then was not what the building looked like, but whether its foundations could stand the buffeting of the wind and the rising water level caused by the flood. The unseen part, the foundations, proved their value then.

The danger with familiarity is that it robs so many stories of their power. This is a case in point. We all think we know the story, and we think we know what the story is about. We tell it in Junior Church lessons, preach about it in worship, and most could sing a chorus about it. But so often we get it wrong. We misinterpret it to make it more comfortable for us. Too often the story is interpreted as the house built on sand representing the unbeliever whilst the house built on the rock represents the believer. That enables us all to go on our way feeling very comfortable and secure in the knowledge that because we are believers we are alright.

But that is not what Jesus said. The contrast in the story is not between those who believe and those who do not but between those who hear Jesus' teaching yet do nothing about it, and those who hear it and allow it to shape them as people. They act upon it, respond to it; take it so seriously that it changes the people they are.

That is far more challenging to us all, especially as we come to the end of our studies in this magnificent sermon. In the story both groups of people, Jesus says, 'hear these words of mine'. They are both members of the visible community of his followers. But the difference is that only some of them put the teaching into practice. Hearing, even believing in some intellectual and shallow way is no substitute for doing something about what we hear. Ironically, when we really hear we begin to really know; and when we really know we have to really do something about it. So the question is whether we have really heard this teaching, whether we really know its truth and if so whether we are going to allow it to shape the people we are. If we do, Jesus says, we will be like a man who built his house on a rock.

Conclusion
Matthew 7: 28-29

The great irony in Matthew's account is that when the sermon was complete, after Jesus had presented the hearers with such choices they were amazed at His teaching, but they did not do anything about it!

One suspects that even though the teaching was delivered to the disciples, during the sermon the crowds gathered. What He said amazed them. It was so unlike anything they had ever heard before. Their own teachers of the law were the ones who were supposed to have authority in these matters. But there was an intrinsic authority with Jesus. Yet it evoked amazement, even admiration, but it did not make them His disciples. They did not, as far as we know, begin to follow Him; nor did they yield their wills to the will of the Father. They may have been pleased with Jesus when the sermon ended. They may even have shook His hand and said that they found it very interesting! But they still had lives built on sand. It need not be so for us.

MET
Methodist Evangelicals Together

Our vision is to fulfil 'Our Calling' and the 'Priorities' of the Methodist Church as we
- uphold the authority of scripture
- seek spiritual renewal
- pray for revival
- spread scriptural holiness
- emphasise the centrality of the cross

MET is the *biggest independent organisation* in British Methodism today

MET is for every *Methodist who shares our vision*

MET is about *the partnership of the Gospel* to proclaim Jesus as Lord. Our partners include:
- Cliff College
- Ignite Revival Network
- Easter People and its successor ECG
- Share Jesus International

MET ensures *the evangelical view is represented* in our Church

Join MET and…
- engage with other evangelical Methodists in prayer and action
- add your voice to over 2,000 others at all levels and in all aspects of the Methodist Church and beyond
- participate in national and local events – conferences, holidays, forums for prayer, debate, learning, worship, new experiences
- receive MET's magazine to be inspired and equipped

We're better together,
so join MET today!

Find us at www.met-uk.org
or write to us $^{c}/_{o}$ Moorley's Print & Publishing
23 Park Road, Ilkeston, Derbys DE7 5DA
who will pass on your valued enquiry.